769 Movies

YOU MUST SEE

BEFORE YOUR

100th Birthday

769 Movies

You Must See

Before Your

100th Birthday

Joseph A. Bonelli

with

Joyce I. Bonelli

SUNSTONE PRESS

SANTA FE

Sunstone books may be purchased for educational, business, or sales promotional use.
For information please write: Special Markets Department, Sunstone Press,
P.O. Box 2321, Santa Fe, New Mexico 87504-2321.
Printed on acid-free paper
∞

eBook 978-1-61139-670-6

Library of Congress Cataloging-in-Publication Data

Names: Bonelli, Joseph A., 1942- author. | Bonelli, Joyce I., 1942- author.

Title: 769 movies you must see before your 100th birthday / Joseph A.
    Bonelli with Joyce I. Bonelli.
Description: Santa Fe : Sunstone Press, [2022] | Includes bibliographical
    references. | Summary: "A personal guide to 769 movies considered
    classic and gems by Joseph and Joyce Bonelli"-- Provided by publisher.
Identifiers: LCCN 2022011843 | ISBN 9781632933782 (paperback) | ISBN
    9781611396706 (epub)
Subjects: LCSH: Motion pictures--Reviews. | Motion pictures--Catalogs.
Classification: LCC PN1998 .B616 2022 | DDC 791.43/75--dc23
LC record available at https://lccn.loc.gov/2022011843

WWW.SUNSTONEPRESS.COM
SUNSTONE PRESS / POST OFFICE BOX 2321 / SANTA FE, NM 87504-2321 /USA
(505) 988-4418 / FAX (505) 988-1025

Dedication

To our son Damon and our daughter-in-law Dana; and our granddaughters, Sophia and Samantha. And our non-human friends, Janet, Ming-Yow, and Ellie. The first two alive only in memory.

And finally, to Juan Duval, Joe's stepfather, an early pioneer in the movie business in Hollywood and Latin America, whose bio, *The Caballero from Catalonia* was published by Sunstone Press in 2019.

Contents

1
Movie Rating Primer

WHY THIS BOOK?

It's a refresher checklist for old-time movie buffs and an eye-opening checklist for the newly-hatched movie lover who is just discovering the marvel of movies, the supreme art form of the modern era.

A "think-list" for movie scholars and historians nominating new titles for "classic" status. I leave the debunking of long-accepted classics that don't deserve that status now because they are dated and boring to others. A list of movies to save for posterity.

This book could also serve as a supplementary text in a cinema class or a movie discussion group.

Perhaps most importantly, it's "challenge lists" for intellectually curious high school and college students, whether Advanced Placement or not, who want to know what kinds of "old" movies might still be of interest and speak to their generation. Believe! Gems are there. Search yours out.

Most movie reviewers use a rating scale of ½ stars (poor) to 4 stars (classic). All movies in my listings will either be 3.0's or 3.5's ("Gems") or 4.0 ("Classics") using my own ratings.

For many famous classic movies, such as "The African Queen" or "Four Feathers" (the 1939 Alexander Korda version) or "The Searchers," my ratings will be the same as that of most reviewers or film historians. But I think that movies like "True Grit" (1969), "Black Rain" (1989), "Hacksaw Ridge" (2016), and "A United Kingdom" (2017) deserve immediate classic status. Reviewers, in my opinion, are too stingy awarding classic status, especially to movies outside the traditional movie establishment.

Some movie reviewers rate movies on their intellectual content, social consciousness or political correctness. To me, a classic movie is not just a neat story told well, it is a movie that knocks your socks off emotionally. It is also a movie you can enjoy seeing again and again.

Some movie reviewers rate movies on their 'artiness.' I despise pretentious movies. To me, "Some Like It Hot" is sophisticated humor while "Last Year at Marienbad" is pretentious. And I understand French.

Some reviewers say they can help you understand or decode the message of the movie. If you can't understand a movie—you are watching the wrong movie. You should look at my genre (category) listings for ideas for different types of movies. There's lots of magic worlds out there for all tastes.

On the subject of 'messages' in movies, I recall an early movie mogul saying, "If you gotta message, use Western Union."

I do not define a movie as a classic just because it is important and famous in the history of cinema unless it is a watchable classic for today's audiences. Sorry to disappoint film historians but movies like "Battleship Potemkin" and "Zero pour Conduite" are not on my lists.

Movie ratings are subjective opinions propounded by people called movie reviewers or critics whose opinions once developed are set down on stone tablets. My ratings of movies come not from my academic University of Southern California Cinema School knowledge but from my 72 years of being a movie lover. Most of the movies on these lists I have seen over again within the last 20 years. And I was able to discuss them with a highly educated and opinionated movie lover—my collaborator—who herself was a movie lover before me. The result has been a sort of vetting process; looking not necessarily for the famous—but for those that will give you grand memories.

Remember, this little tome is mostly about "lists." There are no traditional movie reviews here. If you want to know about plot, setting, actors, etc. of a specified movie, you need to go to Leonard Maltin, *VideoHound's Golden Movie Retriever,* Arthur Knight, Richard Schickel, Pauline Kael, Roger Ebert, Judith Crist, etc. (See also my "References" section.)

Note that, in discussing famous movies, I give the year the movie was made along with the title for some of the entries. It's important to know that date; some movie "stories" have been made many times. For example, there are five versions of "Four Feathers" but the 1939 version is considered the best. No one (yet) has tried to make another version of "The African Queen" or "The Searchers."

Beware of movie titles because they are not protected by copyright (only intellectual content is). There is a Japanese movie called "Black Rain" (1989) which is not of course the same as Ridley Scott's "Black Rain" (of that same year). There is also a 2009 Japanese movie called "The Uninvited" which has nothing to do with the classic 1947 ghost tale of that same name. There are not a lot of these anomalies—but it is good to know about them. Likewise, you may find some movie you're interested in that is not listed in a reference book. It happens, especially with foreign movies trying to break into the American market or with TV productions. Or maybe the reviewers can't keep up (or don't choose to) with the volume of movies being produced. You can always access a title via Internet on the IMDb (Internet Movie Database).

My master movie list will give you the release date for all movies whether or not a second version has been made. It is a piece of useful information and gives you a historical reference frame. The list will also give you a rating (my own) for that movie.

To clarify, a traditional movie review will give you two things: an overall rating on the movie's excellence expressed in (1/2 to 4) stars, and information on the plot (the story). This will include all kinds of miscellaneous information and opinions the reviewer thinks you need to know to make up your mind whether to see the movie or not.

Look upon this as a socially useful function because there are jillions of movies out there and most of them are junk. If you like junk, read no further and enjoy. Reading reviews enables you to separate the gems from the junk—at least to a certain extent. But, it's not an easy process; you must work at it. Reviewers (including myself) have their biases and preferences. Your task is to adjust to those by filtering the information they give you in coming up with winners (movies you really like). If you've dozed or "didn't get it" in the last two movies you picked, you had better get a new reviewer. Try my lists (see self-test next section).

To repeat, this book is about lists of movie ratings sometimes colloquially called "bucket lists." It does not contain traditional reviews; however, there is a "Flick-Notes" section (Chapter 4) that is keyed to a movie's particular "Alpha-numeric" which provides miscellaneous information on some of the movies in the master list. (These are identified by an asterisk.) Some of these highlighted movies are those which critics panned but audiences loved such as "The Russians are Coming, The Russians are Coming" and "Dirty Dancing." I explain how critics went wrong and movie patrons "outvoted" them.

You can consider this book a hyped-up "bucket list" if you wish. Don't think the book title is all hype though, because I have a cousin, Jack, with whom I discuss movies and movie stars. Jack is 101 years old. This book will help you make memorable movie memories of your own.

How to Tell if This Book is for You (Self-test)

By now you probably know all you want to know about movie ratings and reviews. Think about a few of your favorite movies (not the well-known classics like "Casablanca," "The African Queen" or "Jaws," but those lesser known movies you would rate as classics or highly exceptional. Are they rated 4 stars by the movie critics? Or even a 3.5? Likely not. You will be surprised how few "4's" there are relative to the total number of movies reviewed. And few 3.5's. Reviewers are stingier here than they should be. Check my lists. This should quickly tell you if I've given it a rating that is closer to your liking than the conventional critics. Try this for a couple of movies and if you like the results, then maybe we have found each other. My list has 336 Classics and 433 Gems, for a total of 769 movies. How did I come up with this number? I simply remembered all the best movies I and my collaborator had ever seen; then we spent years hunting for new ones. I don't claim to have gotten them all, nor do I expect you will like all my picks. Roll the dice, roll the flick.

If you still don't find some of your favorite movies on my lists, then there are still two possibilities. First, we don't have the same tastes, or second, I have never seen your movies. There's so many out there, and as the White Rabbit in Lewis Caroll's *Alice in Wonderland* says, "There's so little time."

If you have some favorite movie(s) whose correct title you cannot remember, then check my "Category" lists to see if this prompts your memory.

In Chapter 3 (Movies by Category) I have identified three "Top Pick" choices with asterisks. These three choices within each genre are either the "best of the best of the best" or at least representatives of that genre. If the categories are small only one or two choices may be identified. These "Top Pick" choices are indicated with asterisks in Chapter 2, Master Movie List.

2

Master Movie List:
(Classics and Gems in Chronological Order for Each)

"A"

Classics	Year
The Adventures of Robin Hood	1938
Arsenic and Old Lace	1944
The Adventures of Ichabod and Mr. Toad	1949
The African Queen	1951
An American in Paris	1951
Along the Great Divide	1951
Androcles and the Lion	1952
Around the World in 80 Days	1956
American Graffiti	1973
All the President's Men	1976
Apocalypse Now	1979
Alien	1979
The Accused	1988
Always	1989
The Abyss – Special Edition	1989
The Addams Family	1991
Amistad*	1997
Akeelah and the Bee	2006

Australia		2008
Avatar		2009
Argo		2012
All the Money in the World		2017

Gems	Rating	Year
Annie Oakley	3.0	1935
Above Suspicion	3.0	1943
Along Came Jones*	3.0	1945
Angel and the Badman	3.0	1947
Abbot and Costello Meet Frankenstein	3.0	1948
Alice in Wonderland	3.0	1951
African Lion	3.0	1955
Anastasia	3.0	1956
Attack	3.0	1956
Auntie Mame	3.0	1958
Anatomy of a Murder	3.5	1959
The Adventures of Huck Finn	3.5	1960
Attack on the Iron Coast	3.0	1968
The Assassination Bureau	3.5	1969
Alice's Restaurant	3.0	1969
The Aristocats	3.0	1970
An American Werewolf in London	3.0	1981
Amadeus	3.0	1984
Adventures in Babysitting	3.5	1987

Addams Family Values	3.5	1993
Attack on Leningrad	3.0	2009
Alien Covenant	3.0	2017

"B"

Classics	Year
The Big Trail	1930
The Bride of Frankenstein	1935
Bringing Up Baby	1938
Beau Geste	1939
Ball of Fire	1941
The Big Sleep	1946
Broken Arrow*	1950
Brigadoon	1954
Bridge on the River Kwai	1957
Bell, Book, and Candle	1958
Breakfast at Tiffany's	1961
Butch Cassidy and the Sundance Kid	1969
The Battle of Britain*	1969
Bednobs and Broomsticks	1971
Blazing Saddles	1974
Bite the Bullet	1975
Buddy Holly Story	1978
The Blues Brothers	1980

Blade Runner*		1982
Back to the Future		1985
Big Trouble in Little China*		1986
Black Rain*		1989
Beauty and the Beast		1991
The Black Book		2006
Blade Runner (Director's Cut)		2006
The Blind Side		2009
Bridge of Spies		2015
Birth of the Dragon		2017
Bel Canto		2018

Gems	Rating	Year
The Black Swan	3.5	1942
Back to Bataan	3.5	1943
Bataan	3.5	1943
Broadway Rhythm	3.0	1944
Black Narcissus	3.5	1946
Black Arrow	3.5	1948
Beast from 20,000 Fathoms	3.5	1953
Blood Alley	3.5	1955
Bad Day at Black Rock	3.5	1955
The Benny Goodman Story	3.5	1955
The Brave One	3.0	1956
The Bravados	3.0	1958
Bridge to the Sun	3.5	1961

The Birds	3.5	1963
Becket	3.0	1964
The Best Man	3.0	1964
Beneath the Planet of the Apes	3.5	1970
Battle of the Planet of the Apes	3.5	1973
A Bridge Too Far	3.0	1977
Buck Rogers in the 25th Century	3.5	1979
The Bugs Bunny/Roadrunner Movie	3.0	1979
The Black Stallion	3.0	1979
The Big Red One	3.5	1980
Battle Beyond the Stars	3.5	1980
The Best Little Whorehouse in Texas	3.0	1982
Beverly Hills Cop	3.0	1984
The Big Easy	3.5	1987
Big	3.5	1988
Back to the Future II	3.5	1989
Back to the Future III	3.5	1990
Backdraft	3.5	1991
Buffy the Vampire Slayer	3.5	1992
The Bourne Identity	3.5	2002
Bewitched	3.0	2005
Big Game	3.0	2015
Black Panther	3.5	2018
Bad Reputation	3.0	2018
Bohemian Rhapsody	3.5	2018

"C"

Classics	Year
The Count of Monte Cristo	1934
The Charge of the Light Brigade	1936
Casablanca	1942
A Christmas Carol	1951
Captain Horatio Hornblower	1951
The Crimson Pirate	1952
The Cassandra Crossing	1957
The China Syndrome	1979
Congo*	1995
Crouching Tiger, Hidden Dragon	2000
Crazy Rich Asians	2018

Gems	Rating	Year
Captain Blood	3.5	1935
Captain Courageous	3.0	1937
The Cat People	3.5	1942
Cabin in the Sky	3.5	1943
The Canterville Ghost	3.5	1944
The Captain from Castile	3.5	1947
The Cruel Sea	3.5	1953
The Creature from the Black Lagoon	3.5	1954
The Courtmartial of Billy Mitchell	3.5	1955
China Gate	3.5	1957

Chushingura	3.5	1962
Charade	3.5	1963
Cheyenne Autumn	3.5	1964
Cool Hand Luke	3.0	1967
Chitty, Chitty, Bang, Bang	3.0	1968
Catlow	3.5	1971
Carrie	3.5	1976
Cross of Iron	3.5	1977
The Changeling	3.5	1979
Clash of the Titans	3.5	1981
Chariots of Fire	3.5	1981
Cocoon	3.5	1985
Crocodile Dundee	3.5	1986
Chuck Berry: Hail Hail Rock 'n' Roll	3.5	1987
Conagher	3.0	1991
Clueless	3.5	1995
Chicken Run	3.5	2000
Chronicles of Narnia	3.0	2006
Captain Phillips	3.5	2014
Castles in the Sky	3.0	2015

"D"

Classics	Year
David Copperfield	1935
Dodge City	1939
Dumbo	1941
The Day the Earth Stood Still	1951
The Desert Fox	1951
Deadline, U.S.A.	1952
Donovan's Reef*	1963
Dr. Strangelove	1964
Dr. Zhivago	1965
Dirty Harry	1972
The Deer Hunter*	1978
Dirty Dancing*	1987
The Dead Pool	1988
Dances with Wolves	1990
Darkest Hour	2017

Gems	Rating	Year
Destination Tokyo	3.0	1943
Down to the Sea in Ships	3.0	1949
Destination Moon*	3.0	1950
The Desert Rats	3.0	1953
The Dam Busters	3.5	1954
The Defiant Ones	3.0	1958
Darby O'Gill and the Little People	3.5	1959

The Devil's Disciple	3.5	1959
Dr. No	3.5	1962
Diamonds are Forever	3.5	1971
Dersu Uzala	3.5	1974
Dark Star	3.5	1974
Die Hard	3.5	1988
The Disappearance of Garcia Lorca	3.0	1986
Do the Right Thing	3.0	1989
Dante's Peak	3.5	1997
Deep Impact	3.0	1998
The Day After Tomorrow	3.5	2004
Duma	3.5	2005
Dunkirk	3.5	2017

"E"

Classics	**Year**
The Enforcer (Bogey)	1951
The Exorcist	1973
The Enforcer	1976
The Eagle Has Landed	1977
The Empire Strikes Back	1980
E.T.: The Extraterrestrial	1982
The Emerald Forest*	1985
Escape from Sobibor	1987
Everest (IMAX)*	1996

Gems	Rating	Year
El Cid	3.0	1961
El Dorado	3.0	1967
Escape from the Planet of the Apes	3.5	1971
Enter the Dragon	3.5	1973
Escape to Witch Mountain	3.5	1975
The Eiger Sanction	3.5	1975
Escape to Athena	3.0	1979
Eraser	3.5	1996
Elf	3.5	2003
Everest	3.0	2015
The Eagle Huntress	3.0	2016
Eddie the Eagle	3.0	2016

"F"

Classics	Year
The Four Feathers	1939
Fantasia	1940
Friendly Persuasion	1956
Father Goose	1964
Flight of the Phoenix	1966
Fahrenheit 451	1967
The Four Musketeers	1975
Farewell My Lovely	1975
Flash Gordon	1980

Fellowship of the Ring		2001
The First Grader		2010

Gems	Rating	Year
42nd Street	3.0	1933
49th Parallel	3.5	1941
Flying Tigers	3.0	1942
The Fighting Seabees*	3.5	1944
The Flame and the Arrow	3.5	1950
Flying Leathernecks	3.0	1951
From Here to Eternity	3.0	1953
Forbidden Planet	3.5	1956
Flame Over India	3.5	1959
From Russia with Love	3.5	1963
For Your Eyes Only	3.5	1981
Fast Times at Ridgemont High	3.0	1982
Flashdance	3.0	1983
Footloose	3.5	1984
Fern Gully	3.5	1992
The Forgotten Kingdom	3.0	2013
42: The Jackie Robinson Story	3.0	2013
Finding Altamira	3.5	2016
Ford vs. Ferrari	3.5	2019

"G"

Classics	Year
Gone with the Wind	1939
Gunga Din	1939
The Grapes of Wrath	1940
The Ghost and Mrs. Muir	1947
Guys and Dolls	1955
The Guns of Navarone	1961
The Great Escape	1963
The Godfather	1972
Grease	1978
The Gods Must Be Crazy	1981
Ghostbusters	1984
Gremlins	1984
Glory	1989
Gladiator	2000
The Golden Compass	2007
Guernica*	2016
The Great Wall	2017
Go Back to China	2019

Gems	Rating	Year
The Golddiggers of 1933	3.0	1933
Gentlemen Prefer Blondes	3.0	1953
The Girl Can't Help It	3.0	1956
Giant	3.0	1956

Gunfight at OK Corral	3.5	1957
Gigi	3.5	1958
Goldfinger	3.5	1964
Guns at Batasi	3.5	1964
The Glass Bottom Boat	3.5	1966
The Great Waldo Pepper	3.5	1975
Go Tell the Spartans	3.0	1978
Gandhi	3.5	1982
The Good Fight	3.5	1983
Good Morning Vietnam	3.5	1987
The Gods Must Be Crazy II	3.5	1989
Ghostbusters II	3.5	1989
Ghost	3.5	1990
Gettysburg	3.5	1993
Geronimo: An American Legend	3.5	1993
Goldeneye	3.5	1995
The Ghost and the Darkness	3.5	1996
George of the Jungle	3.0	1997
The Guardian	3.5	2006
Gravity	3.0	2013
Green Book	3.5	2018

"H"

Classics	Year
Henry V	1944
Harvey	1950
High Noon	1952
Hondo	1953
Hatari*	1962
Hair	1979
Hamburger Hill	1987
Harry Potter and the Sorcerer's Stone	2001
Howl's Moving Castle	2004
Heidi	2007
Hidden Figures	2016
Hacksaw Ridge	2016

Gems	Rating	Year
His Girl Friday	3.0	1940
The Heiress	3.5	1949
His Majesty O'Keefe	3.5	1953
Heaven Knows Mr. Allison	3.5	1957
Houseboat	3.0	1958
Hound of the Baskervilles	3.0	1959
Heller in Pink Tights	3.5	1960
Hell is for Heroes	3.0	1962
High Wind in Jamaica	3.5	1965

How to Murder Your Wife	3.0	1965
Harper	3.0	1966
Hombre	3.5	1967
High Plains Drifter	3.5	1972
The Hobbit (Animated)	3.0	1978
Harry Potter and The Chamber of Secrets	3.5	2002
Harry Potter and The Prisoner of Azkaban	3.5	2004
Hidalgo	3.5	2004
Harry Potter and The Goblet of Fire	3.5	2005
Harlem Globetrotters, The Team That Changed the World	3.0	2005
Hoot	3.5	2006
Harry Potter and The Order of the Phoenix	3.5	2007
Harry Potter and The Half-Blood Prince	3.5	2009
Harry Potter and The Deathly Hallows, Part I	3.5	2010
Harry Potter and The Deathly Hallows, Part II	3.5	2011
Harriet	3.5	2019

"I"

Classics	Year
Ivanhoe	1952
Invasion of the Body Snatchers	1956
The Incredible Shrinking Man	1957
The Inn of the Sixth Happiness	1958
In the Heat of the Night	1967

Iron Monkey		1993
Independence Day		1996
Ice Age		2002
The Imitation Game		2014

Gems	Rating	Year
It Happened One Night	3.5	1934
I Married a Witch	3.5	1942
I Walked with a Zombie	3.5	1943
I Know Where I'm Going	3.5	1945
Island in the Sky	3.5	1953
It Came From Beneath the Sea	3.5	1955
The Invisible Boy	3.5	1957
Is Paris Burning?	3.5	1960
Inherit the Wind	3.5	1960
Islands of the Blue Dolphins	3.0	1964
The Ipcress File	3.5	1965
In Like Flint	3.5	1967
Indiana Jones and The Temple of Doom	3.5	1984
Into the Night	3.5	1985
Indiana Jones and The Last Crusade	3.5	1989
Indiana Jones and The Kingdom of the Crystal Skull	3.5	2008
In Dubious Battle	3.0	2017
In Harm's Way	3.5	2017

"J"

Classics	Year
The Jungle Book	1942
Johnny Belinda	1948
Journey to the Center of the Earth	1959
Judgement at Nuremberg	1961
Jaws	1975
Jurassic Park	1993
Jurassic Park III	2001
Jurassic World	2015
Jurassic World: Fallen Kingdom	2017

Gems	Rating	Year
Juarez	3.0	1939
Julius Caesar	3.5	1953
Johnny Guitar	3.5	1954
Johnny Tremaine	3.0	1957
Jungle Book (animated)	3.0	1967
Japan's Longest Day	3.0	1967
The Journey of Natty Gann	3.5	1985
Jewel of the Nile	3.5	1985
Jumpin' Jack Flash	3.0	1986

"K"

Classics	Year
King Kong	1933
King Solomon's Mines*	1950
Kim	1950
The King and I	1956
Khartoum*	1966
Kiki's Delivery Service	1989

Gems	Rating	Year
Knock on Wood	3.0	1954
Kings Go Forth	3.5	1958
Klute	3.0	1971
Kagemusha	3.0	1980
Kindergarten Cop	3.5	1990
K-2	3.5	1992
King of Masks	3.5	1999
The King's Speech	3.5	2010

"L"

Classics	Year
The Lives of a Bengal Lancer	1935

Lawrence of Arabia   1962

Little Big Man   1970

Logan's Run   1976

Ladyhawke   1985

Laputa: Castle in the Sky   1986

Last of the Mohicans*   1992

A League of Their Own   1992

The Lost World: Jurassic Park   1997

Lilo and Stitch   2002

Lincoln   2012

Gems	Rating	Year
Last of the Mohicans*	3.0	1936
The Life of Emile Zola	3.5	1937
Lady Eve	3.0	1941
The Lavender Hill Mob	3.5	1951
The Lady Killers	3.5	1955
The Lost World	3.0	1960
The Longest Day	3.5	1962
The Land That Time Forgot	3.5	1975
Little Lord Fauntleroy	3.5	1980
Lion of the Desert	3.5	1981
The Last Starfighter	3.5	1984
Lethal Weapon	3.0	1987
The Living Daylights	3.5	1987
License to Kill	3.5	1989

Last of the Dogmen	3.5	1995
The Last Samurai	3.5	2003
Lilo and Stitch 2	3.5	2005
Las Sandinistas	3.0	2018
Linda Ronstadt: The Sound of My Voice	3.5	2019
Little Women	3.5	2019

"M"

Classics	Year
Mutiny on the Bounty	1935
The Maltese Falcon	1941
Mighty Joe Young	1949
Mogambo	1953
The Music Man	1962
The Miracle Worker	1962
My Fair Lady	1964
Mary Poppins	1964
A Man Called Horse*	1970
Magnum Force	1973
The Man Who Would Be King	1975
Midway*	1976
Moonstruck	1987
My Neighbor Totoro	1988
Midnight Run	1988
Mississippi Burning	1988

	Year
Mountains of the Moon	1990
Mars Attacks	1996
Men in Black	1997
Men in Black II	2002
Men in Black III	2012

Gems	Rating	Year
Mr. Deeds Goes to Town	3.5	1936
My Man Godfrey	3.5	1936
Mr. Smith Goes to Washington	3.5	1939
Major Barbara	3.0	1941
Madame Curie	3.0	1943
The Master of Ballantrae	3.5	1953
The Malta Story	3.5	1953
The Man from Laramie	3.5	1955
Mister Roberts	3.5	1955
Many Rivers to Cross	3.0	1955
The Mouse That Roared	3.5	1959
The Mysterious Island	3.5	1961
Monterey Pop*	3.0	1969
Murder on the Orient Express	3.5	1974
Man with the Golden Gun	3.5	1974
Moonraker	3.5	1976
The Muppet Movie	3.5	1979
The Man from Snowy River	3.5	1982
The Milagro Beanfield War	3.5	1988
The Mighty Quinn	3.0	1989

Malcolm X	3.5	1992
Mrs. Doubtfire	3.5	1993
The Mummy	3.5	1999
Miss Congeniality	3.5	2000
The Mummy Returns	3.5	2001
Monsters, Inc.	3.5	2001
Master and Commander: The Far Side of the World	3.5	2003
Madagascar	3.0	2005
Mongol	3.5	2007
Miracle at St. Anna*	3.5	2008
Mamma Mia	3.5	2008
Monsters vs. Aliens	3.5	2009
The Martian	3.5	2015
Miss Peregrine's Home for Peculiar Children	3.5	2016
Marshall	3.5	2017
Murder on the Orient Express	3.5	2017
The Mountain Between Us	3.0	2017
The Mummy of Tutunkhamun	3.5	2017
The Meg	3.5	2018

"N"

Classics		Year
Nanook of the North		1929
Ninotchka		1939
National Velvet		1944

The Naked Spur		1953
Norma Rae		1979
Nausicaa of the West Wind		1984

Gems	Rating	Year
Naked Jungle	3.5	1954
Night of the Demon	3.5	1957
Network	3.0	1976
Nicholas Nickleby	3.0	1977
Night of the Shooting Stars	3.0	1982
Never Say Never Again	3.0	1983
Night of the Comet*	3.5	1984
Naked Gun	3.0	1988

"O"

Classics	Year
Olympia*	1936
Out of the Past	1947
Oliver Twist	1948
Oklahoma	1955
Operation Crossbow	1965
On Her Majesty's Secret Service*	1969
The Outlaw Josey Wales	1976
Outland	1981
The Ottoman Lieutenant	2017

Gems	Rating	Year
Only Angels Have Wings	3.0	1939
Old Yeller	3.0	1957
Operation Petticoat	3.5	1959
On the Beach	3.5	1959
One Hundred and One Dalmatians	3.5	1961
Our Man Flint	3.5	1966
Octopussy	3.5	1983
Outrageous Fortune	3.5	1987
Outbreak	3.5	1995
On the Basis of Sex	3.5	2018

"P"

Classics	Year
The Prisoner of Zenda	1937
The Prince and the Pauper	1937
Pride and Prejudice	1940
Pinocchio	1940
The Palm Beach Story	1941
Pork Chop Hill	1959
Pollyanna	1960
Panic in the Year Zero	1962
Planet of the Apes	1968
The Producers	1968

Patton	1970
The Poseidon Adventure	1972
Police Academy	1984
Predator	1987
The Princess Bride	1987
Porco Rosso	1992
Princess Mononoke	1997
Pirates of the Caribbean: Curse of the Black Pearl	2003

Gems	**Rating**	**Year**
The Philadelphia Story	3.0	1940
The Princess and the Pirate	3.0	1944
Peter Pan	3.5	1953
The Pride and the Passion	3.0	1957
Paris Blues	3.5	1961
Pressure Point	3.5	1962
The Premature Burial	3.5	1962
The Pink Panther	3.0	1964
The Pink Panther Strikes Again	3.5	1976
The People That Time Forgot	3.5	1977
Pumping Iron	3.0	1977
The Pirates of Penzance	3.5	1983
Prisoners of the Sun	3.5	1991
Pacific Rim	3.5	2013

"Q"

Classics	Year
The Quiet Man	1952

Gems	Rating	Year
Quigley Down Under	3.5	1990
The Queen of Katwe	3.0	2016

"R"

Classics	Year
Red River	1948
River of No Return	1954
Run Silent, Run Deep	1958
The Russians are Coming, The Russians are Coming*	1966
Romeo and Juliet	1968
The Reivers	1969
The Return of a Man Called Horse	1976
Raiders of the Lost Ark	1981
Return of the Jedi	1983
Romancing the Stone	1984
Red Dawn	1984
Ran	1985

Robocop		1987
Return of the King		2003
Race*		2016

Gems	**Rating**	**Year**
The Razor's Edge*	3.5	1946
Rashomon	3.5	1950
Rio Grande	3.0	1950
Rear Window	3.5	1954
Rio Bravo	3.0	1959
Rio Conchos	3.0	1964
Rio Lobo	3.0	1970
Rooster Cogburn	3.0	1975
Rocky	3.0	1976
Return From Witch Mountain	3.5	1978
The Right Stuff	3.5	1983
Repo Man	3.0	1984
Ruthless People	3.0	1986
The Rescuers Down Under	3.0	1990
Renaissance Man	3.5	1994
The Rose Rent	3.5	1996
Roger Corman's Death Race	3.5	2017
Rampage	3.0	2018
Rocketman	3.0	2019

Classics	Year
Snow White and the Seven Dwarves	1937
Stagecoach	1939
The Sea Hawk	1940
Singing in the Rain	1952
The Seven Samurai	1954
The Searchers	1956
The Seventh Seal	1957
The Seventh Voyage of Sinbad	1958
Some Like It Hot	1959
Sink the Bismarck	1960
The Sundowners	1960
The Sound of Music	1965
The Secret of Santa Vittoria	1969
Shaft	1971
Soylent Green	1973
Sting	1973
Secretariat*	1973
Silent Movie	1976
Saturday Night Fever	1977
Star Wars	1977
Superman	1978
Sudden Impact	1983
Starman	1984
Splash	1984

Schindler's List		1993
Starship Troopers		1997
Spirited Away		2001
Shrek		2001
Secondhand Lions		2003
Sahara		2005
The Sentinel		2006
Spotlight		2015
Sully		2016
Snowden		2016
Shaft		2019

Gems	**Rating**	**Year**
Sergeant York	3.0	1941
Sullivan's Travels	3.5	1941
Song of the South	3.0	1946
Secret Garden	3.5	1949
Sailor of the King	3.5	1953
Sansho the Bailiff	3.5	1954
Silver Lode	3.0	1954
The Sheepman	3.0	1958
Swiss Family Robinson	3.0	1960
The Sword of Lancelot	3.5	1963
A Shot in the Dark	3.5	1964
Sands of the Kalahari	3.0	1965
Shalako	3.5	1968

Silent Running	3.0	1971
Serpico	3.5	1973
The Shootist	3.5	1976
Silver Streak	3.5	1976
The Spy Who Loved Me	3.5	1977
The Sea Wolves	3.5	1980
Superman II	3.5	1981
Star Trek II: The Wrath of Khan	3.5	1982
Short Circuit	3.5	1986
Sleepless in Seattle	3.5	1993
Sense and Sensibility	3.5	1995
Seven Years in Tibet	3.5	1997
Sphere	3.5	1998
Saving Private Ryan	3.5	1998
Stuart Little	3.0	1999
Star Wars I: The Phantom Menace	3.5	2000
Shaft	3.5	2000
Surrogates	3.5	2009
Super 8	3.5	2011
7 Days in Entebbe	3.0	2017
Star Wars Episode IX: The Rise of Skywalker	3.5	2019

Classics	Year
Top Hat	1935
Topper	1937
The Thief of Baghdad	1940
30 Seconds Over Tokyo	1944
The Three Caballeros	1945
Treasure Island	1950
The Thing	1951
This Island Earth	1954
20,000 Leagues Under the Sea	1954
The Girl Can't Help It	1956
Teahouse of the August Moon	1956
The Three Faces of Eve	1957
12 Angry Men	1957
3:10 to Yuma	1957
Thunder Road	1958
To Kill a Mockingbird	1962
Tom Jones	1963
Topkapi	1964
That Darn Cat	1965
True Grit	1969
Tora, Tora, Tora	1970
The Three Musketeers	1974
That's Entertainment	1974
The Tamarind Seed	1974

Tommy   1975

Three Days of the Condor   1975

Tootsie   1982

The Terminator   1984

Terminator II: Judgement Day   1991

Thelma and Louise (Special Edition)   1991

Toy Story   1995

Twister   1996

Titanic   1997

The 13th Warrior   1999

The Two Towers   2002

Tears of the Sun   2003

Terminator III: Rise of the Machines   2003

The 33   2015

13 Hours: The Secret Soldiers of Benghazi   2016

12 Strong   2018

Gems	Rating	Year
Topper Returns	3.5	1941
To Have and Have Not	3.5	1944
12 O'clock High	3.0	1949
Them	3.5	1954
20 Million Miles to Earth	3.5	1957
Thunderball	3.5	1965
One Thousand Clowns	3.5	1965
Topaz	3.0	1969
A Touch of Zen	3.5	1971

	Rating	Year
That's Entertainment, Part II	3.5	1976
Time after Time	3.0	1979
Twins	3.5	1988
Total Recall	3.5	1990
Teenage Mutant Ninja Turtles	3.5	1990
True Lies	3.5	1994
12 Monkeys	3.5	1995
Tea with Mussolini	3.5	1999
Thirteen Days	3.5	2000
Toy Story 4	3.0	2019

"U"

Classics	Year
The Uninvited	1947
Used Cars	1980
Under the Tuscan Sun	2003
A United Kingdom*	2017

Gems	Rating	Year
Up Periscope	3.5	1959
Up in Smoke	3.5	1978
Uptown Girls	3.0	2003
The Upside	3.5	2019

"V"

Classics	Year
Vertigo	1958
The Valley of Gwangi*	1969

Gems	Rating	Year
Voyage to the Bottom of the Sea	3.5	1961
A View to a Kill	3.5	1985
Victoria and Abdul	3.0	2017
Valley Girl	3.5	2020

"W"

Classics	Year
The Wizard of Oz	1939
The Wake of the Red Witch	1948
Winchester 73	1950
War of the Worlds	1953
War and Peace	1956
Westside Story	1961
The Wrong Box	1966
Where Eagles Dare	1969
Waterloo	1971
The Wind and the Lion	1975
Where the River Runs Black	1986

Who Framed Roger Rabbit?		1988
We Bought a Zoo		2011

Gems	**Rating**	**Year**
War Arrow	3.5	1953
White Lightning	3.5	1973
Wild Geese	3.5	1978
Wolfen	3.5	1981
The Witches of Eastwick	3.5	1987
Willow	3.5	1988
When Harry Met Sally	3.5	1989
Wind	3.5	1992
Waterworld	3.5	1995
The World is Not Enough	3.5	1999
Winged Migration	3.0	2001
Windtalkers	3.5	2002
Wallace and Grommit: In the Curse of the Were-Rabbit	3.0	2005
The Way Back	3.5	2010
War Horse	3.5	2011
Wolverine	3.0	2013
Wind River	3.5	2016

"X"

Classics	Year
Xanadu	1980
X-Men	2000
X2: X-Men United	2003
X-Men Last Stand	2006
X-Men: Dark Phoenix	2019

Gems	Rating	Year
X-Men: Days of Future Past	3.5	2014

"Y"

Classics	Year
You Can't Take It with You	1938
Young Frankenstein	1974
The Yakuza	1975

Gems	Rating	Year
Yankee Doodle Dandy	3.5	1942
Yojimbo	3.5	1961
You Only Live Twice	3.5	1967
The Yellow Submarine	3.0	1968
You've Got Mail	3.5	1998

Classics	Year
Zulu	1964
Zulu Dawn	1979

Gems	Rating	Year
The Zookeeper's Wife	3.5	2017

3

Movies by Category

Note: Many movies can be placed in more than one genre category; but to keep things simple every movie in the Master Movie List in Chapter 2 will be assigned to just one of the following categories:

1. Adventure

2. Sci-fi

3. Comedy

4. Historical

5. Family

6. Horror

7. Africa

8. Cop

9. Mystery

10. Friendship

11. Children (of all ages)

12. War

13. Courtroom/legal challenge

14. Drama

15. Romance/love stories

16. Screwball comedy

17. Westerns

18. Ghost

19. Politics

20. Japanese (except Miyazaki)

21. Docu-drama

22. Musicals

23. Spanish

24. Fantasy

25. Other Foreign

26. Russian

27. Harry Potter

28. James Bond

29. Disney

30. Miyazaki

31. Dirty Harry

32. Sci-fi/Apes

33. Jurassic Park

34. Indiana Jones

35. Tolkien/Lord of the Rings

36. Star Wars

37. Men in Black

38. X-Men

39. Chinese

For the larger genre/categories, three "top picks" have been asterisked for your convenience. For smaller categories only one or two may be identified. But remember, every movie here is worth viewing. If you do not like my three picks, keep going and discover your own.

ADVENTURE

The Adventures of Robin Hood, Flight of the Phoenix, The Land That Time Forgot, *The Four Feathers, Around the World in 80 Days, The Four Musketeers, The Last Samurai, Last of the Mohicans (1936), Argo, The Flame and the Arrow, The Mysterious Island, Romancing the Stone, The Assassination Bureau, Flame over India, The Man from Snowy River, Seven Years in Tibet, Blood Alley, Gunga Din, Operation Crossbow, The Thief of Bagdad, Big Game, The Great Waldo Pepper, Only Angels Have Wings, 20,000 Leagues Under the Sea, Captain Blood, High Wind in Jamaica, The Prisoner of Zenda, Topkapi, Crocodile Dundee, Hidalgo, The Poseidon Adventure, The Three Musketeers, *The Wind and the Lion, *Ivanhoe, Pirates of the Caribbean: Curse of the Black Pearl, Topaz, Everest (IMAX), Iron Monkey, The Princess and the Pirate, The Sea Wolves, Everest, K-2, The People that Time Forgot, Naked Jungle, Eddie the Eagle, Last of the Mohicans (1992), Quigley Down Under, Mutiny on the Bounty, His Majesty O'Keefe, Down to the Sea in Ships, The Devil's Disciple, The Eiger Sanction, Nanook of the North, Captain Horatio Hornblower, The Ipcress File, Island in the Sky, Captains Courageous, The Count of Monte Cristo, The Sea Hawk, Shaft, Captain Phillips, The Black Arrow, The Bourne Identity, The Black Swan, Birth of the Dragon, The Crimson Pirate, Lost World, Lives of a Bengal Lancer, Last of the Dogmen, Land That Time Forgot, The Mummy of Tutunkhamun, Wind, The Tamarind Seed, The Adventures of Huckleberry Finn, Where the River Runs Black, The Cassandra Crossing, Sahara.

Alien, Forbidden Planet, Surrogates, Flash Gordon, *Avatar, Invasion of the Body Snatchers, Super 8, Sphere, Waterworld, The Incredible Shrinking Man, The Thing, ET: The Extraterrestrial, Back to the Future, Independence Day, This Island Earth, Fahrenheit 451, Buck Rogers in the 25th Century, Journey to the Center of the Earth, The Terminator, Starship Troopers, Battle Beyond the Stars, *Logan's Run, Terminator II: Judgment Day, Silent Running, Back to the Future II, The Last Starfighter, Terminator III: Rise of the Machines, Alien Covenant, Back to the Future III, Outland, Them, The Meg, *The Day the Earth Stood Still, Soylent Green, 20 Million Miles to Earth, Gravity, Destination Moon, Starman, War of the Worlds, The Abyss-Special Edition, The Beast from 20,000 Fathoms, It Came From Beneath the Sea, Star Wars: The Phantom Menace, Star Trek II: The Wrath of Kahn, Total Recall, Blade Runner, The Invisible Boy, Blade Runner 2049.

COMEDY

Arsenic and Old Lace, The Girl Can't Help It, The Philadelphia Story, Up in Smoke, American Graffiti, Ghostbusters II, The Pink Panther, Uptown Girls, *The Addams Family, How to Murder Your Wife, *The Russians are Coming, The Russians are Coming, The Wrong Box, Auntie Mame, Ice Age, Repo Man, Who Framed Roger Rabbit?, Addams Family Values, The Lady Killers, Ruthless People, When Harry Met Sally, Blazing Saddles, Mars Attacks, Some Like it Hot, Young Frankenstein, The Blues Brothers, The Mouse that Roared, Silent Movie, A League of Their Own, Clueless, The Naked Gun, Shrek, Abbot & Costello Meet Frankenstein, *Dr. Strangelove, Operation Petticoat, Silver Streak, Bewitched, Father Goose, Our Man Flint, Topper, In Like Flint, Ghostbusters, Outrageous Fortune, Tom Jones, Jumpin' Jack Flash, Cabin in the Sky, The Producers, Used Cars, Knock on Wood, Lavender Hill Mob, Short Circuit, The Pink Panther Strikes Again, Mrs. Doubtfire, A Shot in the Dark, Topper Returns.

HISTORICAL

Anastasia, Gandhi, Mongol, Bridge of Spies, *Lincoln, Amadeus, The Imitation Game, Castles in the Sky, 42: The Jackie Robinson Story, Life of Emile Zola, Juarez, Green Book, Geronimo: An American Legend, Harriet, Ford vs. Ferrari, Madame Curie.

FAMILY

Alice's Restaurant, Heidi, *The Sundowners, Under the Tuscan Sun, Cocoon, King of Masks, Second Hand Lions, *We Bought a Zoo, Deer Hunter, The Queen of Katwe, Swiss Family Robinson, White Lightning, Elf, The Rievers, Twins, The Witches of Eastwick, *Friendly Persuasion, Renaissance Man, Island of the Blue Dolphins, Nicholas Nickelby, National Velvet, The Brave One, Old Yeller, Thunder Road, Footloose, Akeelah and the Bee, The Blind Side.

HORROR

The Birds, Gremlins, Night of the Comet, An American Werewolf in London, Buffy the Vampire Slayer, I Walked with a Zombie, *Predator, Carrie, The Cat People, *Jaws, Time after Time, Premature Burial, The Creature from the Black Lagoon, The Mummy, Wolfen, Night of the Demon, The Exorcist, The Mummy Returns, The Bride of Frankenstein.

AFRICA

*The African Queen, The Gods Must Be Crazy, *King Solomon's Mines, Sands of the Kalahari, Congo, The Gods Must Be Crazy II, Khartoum, A United Kingdom, Duma, The Ghost and the Darkness, Lawrence of Arabia, Mountains of the Moon, The Forgotten Kingdom, Jewel of the Nile, Mogambo, The First Grader, *Hatari, Lion of the Desert, Black Panther, Guns at Batasi.

COP

*Black Rain, Kindergarten Cop, *Robocop, The Sentinel, Beverly Hills Cop, Miss Congeniality, Shaft, Harper, Lethal Weapon, Police Academy, *Blade Runner, Farewell My Lovely, Klute, Serpico, The Enforcer, The Big Easy, Wind River, Shaft 2019, Mississippi Burning.

MYSTERY

*In the Heat of the Night, *The Maltese Falcon, The Mighty Quinn, Charade, Into the Night, Murder on the Orient Express, Rear Window, Murder on the Orient Express (2017), The Big Sleep, Out of the Past, Hound of the Baskervilles.

FRIENDSHIP

Bite the Bullet, *Dirty Dancing, The Man Who Would be King, Norma Ray, Casablanca, *Johnny Belinda, Midnight Run, Splash, *Donovan's Reef, Kim, Ninotchka, Adventures in Babysitting, Monsters vs. Aliens, In Dubious Battle, The Ottoman Lieutenant, Bel Canto, The Upside, Thelma and Louise.

CHILDREN (OF ALL AGES)

George of the Jungle, *Bedknobs and Broomsticks, Hoot, The Muppet Movie, *Mary Poppins, Chitty Chitty Bang Bang, *The Jungle Book, The Prince and the Pauper, The Bugs Bunny Roadrunner Movie, Toy Story 4, The Jungle Book (animated), Secret Garden, Teenage Mutant Ninja Turtles, Fern Gully, Little Lord Fauntleroy, Toy Story, The Rescuers Down Under, Monsters, Inc., Charlotte's Web.

Apocalypse Now, The Eagle Has Landed, Midway, Tora, Tora, Tora, Above Suspicion, Escape to Athena, Master and Commander: The Far Side of the World, Three Days of the Condor, Attack on Leningrad, Flying Tigers, Miracle at St. Anne's, The Thirteenth Warrior, Bridge on the River Kwai, The Fighting Seabees, Pork Chop Hill, 13 Hours: The Secret Soldiers of Benghazi, *The Battle of Britain, The Guns of Navarone, Patton, Twelve O'Clock High, The Black Book, The Great Escape, The Pride and the Passion, Tea with Mussolini, A Bridge Too Far, *Glory, Run Silent, Run Deep, War and Peace, The Big Red One, Good Morning Vietnam, Sink the Bismarck, Where Eagles Dare, The Captain from Castile, Henry V, Schindler's List, Zulu, China Gate, *Hacksaw Ridge, Sergeant York, Wild Geese, Cross of Iron, Hell is for Heroes, Saving Private Ryan, The Way Back, Destination Tokyo, Is Paris Burning?, Zulu Dawn, The War Horse, Gettysburg, Flying Leathernecks, El Cid, Back to Bataan, Night of the Shooting Stars, The Desert Rats, The Cruel Sea, Panic in Year Zero, Escape from Sobibor, The Charge of the Light Brigade, Windtalkers, 49th Parallel, The Desert Fox, Dunkirk, 12 Strong, Attack, Attack on the Iron Coast, Sailor of the King, Up Periscope, Hamburger Hill, Bataan, The Malta Story.

COURTROOM/LEGAL CHALLENGES

*Amistad, Judgment at Nuremburg, 12 Angry Men, The Court Martial of Billy Mitchell, Prisoners of the Sun, Marshall, On the Basis of Sex, Anatomy of a Murder, Inherit the Wind, The Accused.

DRAMA

Androcles and the Lion, Giant, The Razor's Edge, *Gladiator, Beau Geste, Chariots of Fire, Rocky, The Razor's Edge, Bad Day at Black Rock, The Guardian, *The Secret of Santa Vittoria, The Rose Rent, Becket, Hidden Figures, The Sting, 7 Days in Entebbe, Backdraft, Heaven Knows Mr. Allison, Sully, All the Money in the World, The China Syndrome, Julius Caesar, Snowden, Spotlight, Cool

Hand Luke, The King's Speech, Teahouse of the August Moon, Victoria and Abdul, The Changeling, Major Barbara, The Three Faces of Eve, Black Narcissus, Deadline, USA, Mister Roberts, Twelve Monkeys, The Brothers Karamazov, The Defiant Ones, The Milagro Beanfield War, To Kill a Mockingbird, Do the Right Thing, Die Hard, The Martian, Tootsie, David Copperfield, Dante's Peak, Network, Twister, Malcolm X, Deep Impact, The Outlaw Josey Wales, Titanic, The Miracle Worker, The Day After Tomorrow, *Outbreak, Tears of the Sun, On the Beach, Eraser, River of No Return, The 33, Oliver Twist, The Grapes of Wrath, Red Dawn, To Have and Have Not, Pride and Prejudice, The Godfather, Race, One Thousand Clowns, The Right Stuff, True Lies, Sense & Sensibility, The Heiress, Fast Times at Ridgemont High, Little Women, Kings Go Forth, Pressure Point.

ROMANCE/LOVE STORIES

*Always, From Here to Eternity, The Inn of the Sixth Happiness, Romeo & Juliet, Australia, Gone with the Wind, I Know Where I'm Going, The Wake of the Red Witch, Annie Oakley, The Quiet Man, *Moonstruck, You've Got Mail, Dr. Zhivago, The Glass Bottom Boat, Paris Blues, The Sword of Lancelot, Sleepless in Seattle, Houseboat, The Mountain Between Us, Bridge to the Sun.

SCREWBALL COMEDY

Bringing Up Baby, It Happened One Night, I Married a Witch, Many Rivers to Cross, *Ball of Fire, The Lady Eve, The Palm Beach Story, Gentlemen Prefer Blondes, His Girl Friday, My Man Godfrey.

WESTERNS

Along Came Jones, Hondo, Rio Lobo, High Noon, Angel and the Badman, Hombre, Rooster Cogburn, Rio Grande, The Big Trail, High Plains Drifter, Stagecoach, Johnny Guitar, *Broken Arrow,

Little Big Man, *The Searchers, Silver Lode, Butch Cassidy & The Sundance Kid, A Man Called Horse, Sheepman, Shalako, Catlow, The Man from Laramie, The Shootist, War Arrow, Dances with Wolves, The Return of a Man Called Horse, *True Grit, Heller in Pink Tights, El Dorado, Rio Bravo, The Valley of Gwangi, Cheyenne Autumn, Gunfight at OK Corral, Rio Conchos, Winchester 73, Along the Great Divide, Conagher, Red River, The Naked Spur, 3:10 to Yuma, Dodge City, The Bravadoes.

GHOSTS

The Ghost and Mrs. Muir, Ghost, *The Uninvited, The Canterville Ghost.

POLITICS

All the President's Men, The Best Man, Mr. Smith Goes to Washington, Mr. Deeds Goes to Town, *Thirteen Days.

JAPANESE (EXCEPT MIYAZAKI)

Ran, Rashomon, *Seven Samurai, Chushingura, Sansho the Bailiff, Yojimbo, Kagemusha.

DOCU-DRAMA

The Good Fight, That's Entertainment, *Olympia, Winged Migration, Japan's Longest Day, That's Entertainment II, Pumping Iron, Harlem Globetrotters: The Team That Changed the World, Las Sandinistas.

MUSICALS

An American in Paris, The Golddiggers of 1933, Mamma Mia, The Girl Can't Help It, Brigadoon, Gigi, Oklahoma, Tommy, The Buddy Holly Story, Hair, The Pirates of Penzance, *The Wizard of Oz, Chuck Berry, Hail, Hail, Rock 'n Roll, The King and I, Singing in the Rain, Westside Story, 42nd Street, The Music Man, The Sound of Music, Xanadu, *Guys and Dolls, My Fair Lady, Saturday Night Fever, Yankee Doodle Dandy, *Grease, Monterey Pop, Top Hat, Bad Reputation, Bohemian Rhapsody, The Benny Goodman Story, Flashdance, Rocketman, Linda Ronstadt: The Sound of My Voice, Valley Girl 2020, Broadway Rhythm, The Best Little Whorehouse in Texas.

SPANISH

The Disappearance of Garcia Lorca, Finding Altamira, *Guernica.

FANTASY

*Bell, Book and Candle, Harvey, Superman, The Golden Compass, The Seventh Voyage of Sinbad, *Ladyhawke, Superman II, Roger Corman's Death Race 2050, Big, Miss Peregrine's Home for Peculiar Children, Stuart Little, The Emerald Forest, The Yellow Submarine, The Princess Bride, Voyage to the Bottom of the Sea, Rampage, Clash of the Titans, Pacific Rim, Willow, The Hobbit (Animated), Dark Star.

OTHER FOREIGN

The Eagle Huntress, *The Seventh Seal.

RUSSIAN

Dersu Uzala, *Waterloo.

HARRY POTTER

Harry Potter and the Sorcerer's Stone, Harry Potter and the Goblet of Fire, Harry Potter and the Deathly Hallows Part I, Harry Potter and the Prisoner of Azkaban, Harry Potter and the Chamber of Secrets, Harry Potter and the Order of the Phoenix, Harry Potter and the Deathly Hallows Part II, *Harry Potter and the Prisoner of Azkaban.

JAMES BOND

Doctor No, License to Kill, Living Daylights, Goldfinger, *Diamonds are Forever, The Man with the Golden Gun, The Spy Who Loved Me, Goldeneye, From Russia with Love, Moonraker, Thunderball, *On Her Majesty's Secret Service, For Your Eyes Only, Never Say Never Again, A View to a Kill, Octopussy, The World is Not Enough, You Only Live Twice.

DISNEY

The Adventures of Ichabod and Mr. Toad, Fantasia, African Lion, Johnny Tremaine, The Aristocats, *The Journey of Natty Gann, *Secretariat, Alice in Wonderland, Beauty and the Beast, Lilo and Stitch, Song of the South, Peter Pan, Dumbo, One Hundred and One Dalmations, The Three Caballeros, Pollyanna, Darby O'Gill and the Little People, Pinocchio, Treasure Island, Return from Witch Mountain, Escape to Witch Mountain, Snow White & the Seven Dwarfs, That Darn Cat, Chronicles of Narnia, Lilo & Stitch 2.

MIYAZAKI

Howl's Moving Castle, My Neighbor Totoro, Princess Mononoke, Laputa: Castle in the Sky,Kiki's Delivery Service, Nausicaa of the West Wind, *Spirited Away, Porco Rosso.

DIRTY HARRY

*Dirty Harry, The Enforcer, The Dead Pool, Magnum Force, Sudden Impact.

SCI-FI (APES)

King Kong, Beneath the Planet of the Apes, Battle for the Planet of the Apes, *Planet of the Apes, Mighty Joe Young, Escape from Planet of the Apes, Congo, Conquest of the Planet of the Apes.

JURASSIC PARK

*Jurassic Park, Jurassic World, The Lost World: Jurassic Park, Jurassic World: Fallen Kingdom, Jurassic Park II.

INDIANA JONES

Indiana Jones and the Temple of Doom, *The Raiders of the Lost Ark, Indiana Jones and the Kingdom of the Crystal Skull, Indiana Jones and the Last Crusade.

TOLKIEN/LORD OF THE RINGS

*Fellowship of the Ring, The Two Towers, Return of the King.

STAR WARS

*Star Wars, The Empire Strikes Back, Return of the Jedi, Star Wars I: The Phantom Menace,Star Wars IX: The Rise of Skywalker.

MEN IN BLACK

*Men in Black, Men in Black II, Men in Black III.

X-MEN

*X-Men, X-Men United, X-Men Last Stand, X-Men: Days of Future Past, X-Men: Dark Phoenix, Wolverine.

CHINESE

*Enter the Dragon, Flying Tigers, Blood Alley, A Touch of Zen, The Inn of the Sixth Happiness, Iron Monkey, In Harm's Way 2017, *Go Back to China, Crouching Tiger, Hidden Dragon, *The Great Wall, Big Trouble in Little China, Crazy Rich Asians.

<h1 align="center">4</h1>

<h1 align="center">Flick-Notes
(By Master Movie List,
Alpha-Numeric)</h1>

A-16 / AMISTAD

This engrossing and entertaining movie did not receive the acclaim it was due. It's also an interesting example of a movie transcending genre boundaries. It's "Africa," "Adventure," "History," "Politics," and "Courtroom/Legal Challenges." It's about a slave rebellion and the aftermath on a Spanish slaver named the "Amistad." This is one of history's uncanny ironies: Amistad in Spanish means 'amity/ friendship, etc.' The legal and courtroom strategy on display in this historical movie will surprise you and *should* remind us that our Yankee forefathers were a crafty yet idealistic bunch. Every aware student should see this movie; for every law student this is a must-see movie.

A-22 / Along Came Jones

Loretta Young, Gary Cooper, and Dan Duryea have a good time in this one. When I was in grammar school, one of my buddies was a friend and neighbor to Loretta and took me to her house to introduce me. She was the same gracious lady in real life as she was on the screen. This was in Hollywood in the early fifties.

B-6 / Broken Arrow

This is real southwestern history depicted honestly and accurately about two towering historic figures, Tom Jeffords and Chief Cochise of the Chiricahua Apache. Don't know about the romance part, but it works too.

B-12 / The Battle of Britain

This move was sadly underrated by many film reviewers. Yet, it's a small masterpiece of its kind. It is a historically accurate and interesting account of the early World War II period when British aviators filled the sky with Spitfires to stem the planned Nazi invasion of Britain. British servicemen and private citizens worked together in a massive web of intelligently planned national defense.

B-18 / Blade Runner

Some reviewers panned this movie when it came out and wondered at all the people that seemed smitten with it. Well, it's all about atmosphere and style and swagger. Ridley Scott is the master of atmosphere—who else would "guess" what Los Angeles might look like in the future. And what LA cops might have to do. Good basic sci-fi, done well. If you've seen the later versions, forget them—and start over with the real McCoy.

B-20 / Big Trouble in Little China

The literary source for this movie is Chinese quanqi (tales of wonder). Quanqi meets westerners—and humor. Bizarre, entertaining and fun.

B-21 / Black Rain

See detailed "plot analysis" later in this book (if you're the kind of person that likes to see the jigsaw mechanics of how a complex plot is put together). This "plot analysis" is sort of an abbreviated "movie treatment."

C-8 / Congo

Why didn't some of the critics like this one? It had an intelligent story (Michael Crichton), attractive actors (male, female and primate). Lots of action. Some gruesome scenes, some humor. A knockout story. Maybe the idea we might be able to "talk" to a gorilla freaks the critics out. By the way, the gorilla "art therapy" used in this movie is used in real life at the Jane Goodall Foundation working with traumatized chimps.

D-6 / Donovan's Reef

This is a well-liked rollicking John Wayne/Lee Marvin/John Ford South Sea island production. It deserves even more respect than it garnered. It's a riveting story of three men and the strange things that must be done sometimes in the interest of friendship.

It's about "half-castes" and racial labeling in 1963, which is a far different world than we have today. A world where few white women would willingly associate with half-castes. It's about "reverence" for a lovely young queen and respect for her native culture.

It's about love, caring, generosity and good people. Although Wayne's "caveman" wooing technique and his and Marvin's "friendly fisticuffs" might offend some current day sensibilities, this is a movie not to be missed. Full of life. A good trip.

D-10 / The Deer Hunter

I first saw this movie in a Washington, DC suburban movie theater the year after its release (1978). This was during the Vietnam War. The audience reaction was electric. People were alternately crying, moaning; some were even crying out in anguish. I have seldom seen a movie that so touched people by bridging the gap between the real world and the movie "fantasy world." For many people of that time, this was *the* Vietnam movie. It was about friendship, family, and the survivors coming home.

D-11 / Dirty Dancing

An upper middle-class 17-year-old vacations with her parents in the Catskills where she discovers rock 'n' roll, sex, love, and dance instructor Patrick Swayze. To most critics that's all this movie is about but it's also a coming of age story where Jennifer Grey discovers that some men are decent, and others are dipshits. She learns how to tell the difference and learns a lot about friendship, hypocrisy and hot dancing.

D-17 / DESTINATION MOON

Enjoyable early sci-fi. I was eight when this movie came out (1950). My mother, stepfather and I lived in Hollywood next door to Warner Anderson, star of this movie. A friendly man and good neighbor. The Sunset Strip was two blocks away.

E-7 / THE EMERALD FOREST

Suppose you live on the edge of the Amazon rain forest and your small son is kidnapped by forest natives. Suppose from the other side of the forest curtain you save a child from the awful land where nothing grows, and nothing lives. This is like the "reality dilemma" in "Rashomon." This is a unique fantasy, well thought out and scripted. And great acting by "Boy."

E-9 / EVEREST – IMAX

Though short (less than one hour) this movie has a lot to offer. It was likely originally scripted as a simple mountain climbing film to 'ooh' and 'ah' the audience with mountain scenery with those sensational cameras. It does that, but something happened on the way to the summit. Massive catastrophe strikes an earlier summit party and our crew pitches in to aid in the rescue and cleanup. On the verge of having to go back down the mountain, the weather suddenly clears so they send two of their strongest climbers up for a summit try. They make it. One of them, a personable young lady (a technical rock climber turned mountain climber) was the first Spanish female to summit. Viva España!

F-11 / The First Grader

This is an engrossing tale of present-day Kenya. A village elder wants to enter school so he can learn to read and understand the new world he inhabits. He had been Mau Mau in his youth, following his tribe's elders. Consequently, he spent most of his adult life in a British prison. And now he must face another implacable enemy—the school bureaucrats of his own people.

F-15 / The Fighting Seabees

This is a good 'ole John Wayne flick and one of the better movies made about World War II in the Pacific. I know what the Seabees did for our country from a primary source; my uncle Louie was at Dutch Harbor in the Aleutians when the Japanese attacked there (part of the Battle of Midway). More importantly, he was with the first waves of Marines to hit the beach at Peleliu. A little-known battle where the Japanese first showed their new tactics—which later made Okinawa hell on earth.

G-16 / Guernica

This is a well-done war story about a little town with no strategic military value in the Basque country during the Spanish Civil War. As the story unfolds you get to know some of the locals and "political soldiers" of all stripes, even Franquistas. Yet the massive air attack when it comes is stunning. The Nazi's were tuning up their air attack tactics for World War II. But why here? Because Franco and Hitler were good at delivering symbolic messages. There was an old tree in Guernica under which several hundred years ago the rights of Basques were accepted by the powers that were. A new message was being delivered.

H-5 / HATARI

Large parts of this multi-genre movie are screwball comedy at its finest. Superb script by Leigh Brackett who, unknown to movie fans, was one of the early great writers of the Golden Age of science fiction. It's about family, romance, adventure, comedy and has some of the most breathtaking African animal photography you'll ever see. And Mancini's music, especially his 'Baby Elephant Walk' theme, should bring a smile from even the Grinch himself.

H-11 / HACKSAW RIDGE

This bloody movie tells it just like it was on Okinawa. Someone on the production staff must have read E.B. Sledge's military classic "With the Old Breed at Peleliu and Okinawa." As a war/anti-war movie, as the personal odyssey of an extraordinary human being, this movie was done right.

K-2 / KING SOLOMON'S MINES

This movie deviates in plot considerably from H. Rider Haggard's book (which had no women in the plot). However, for me, it comes closest to the spirit of that book (several versions followed this movie and one preceded it). In this case, the bold reworking or "modernizing" of the plot paid off as Deborah Kerr and Stewart Granger journeyed together in search of the legendary mine. "Modern" psychology (but not Freudian claptrap) was brought to bear on character motivation. Spectacular scenery/great adventure. And those drums!

K-5 / KHARTOUM

The critics didn't like this movie when it came out way back in 1966. "Dull history / talky spectacle" they called it. I think their biases were showing. This is one of the most underrated historical epics Hollywood ever made. It was historically accurate and sensitive to all viewpoints in this Sudan cultural battle between the Anglo/Egyptian forces under General "Chinese" Gordon and the Islamic religious leader, the "Mahdi." The Mahdi, for those interested in the current day "confusion" in the Middle East, was a sort of early Al Quada figure.

L-7 / LAST OF THE MOHICANS, 1992

The hero of this movie is nothing like the character in the James Fenimore Cooper novels. Never mind that this movie is great on its own merits. It's typical of movies where either some of the plot is borrowed from a famous book or some of the characteristics of that book's famous protagonist is used. In this case, John Day Lewis got "Hawkeye's" long rifle—and it served him quite nicely.

M-9 / A MAN CALLED HORSE

This is solid western history and perhaps the best cinematic portrayal of Native American culture ever done (and the entire population of a current day reservation were the actors). An English lord, sightseeing in early America, is captured by "Yellow Hand" Sioux band. The chief, because he likes this crazy white man's spirit, saves his life by calling him "Shunkawakan" (horse). Since this "joke" allows the lord to live (as a household servant) he has a future. By proving himself, he becomes a Yellow Hand leader. Stranger than fiction. Followed by a well-done sequel.

M-12 / MIDWAY

This is a Hollywood blockbuster with loads of big-name acting talent that was badly treated by the critics as having trite dialogue and a "sidebar romance" between Charlton Heston's son and his "Enemy Alien" incarcerated young Japanese-American sweetheart. (A sidebar more likely to be popular today than in 1976.)

Yet, in spite of that, this is an enjoyable movie and historically accurate, showing how "Intelligence" is the keyword in the term "Military Intelligence." And how we "predicted" what the Japanese would do, thus tipping the scales in our favor, in this, the turning point battle in the Pacific.

M-31 / MONTEREY POP

This is one of the earliest and best "rock" movies. And yours truly was there for all three days—which netted me a quick one-second "walk-by" part in this movie. Perhaps the first time a reviewer rated a movie that he or she was in? The experience was exceptional— and the moviemakers did a fine job in recording that experience.

This a World War II war movie with a different point of view. Made by Spike Lee, it portrays life in wartime Italy as experienced by a small group of Black American soldiers. (Yes folks, our army was segregated back then.) They feel they are treated better there than back at home. Worth seeing, but not for the faint of heart.

N-12 / Night of the Comet

Horror is not my favorite genre, but this zombie movie stands out for its intelligence and humor. It's about a guy and two Valley girls. Why did everyone turn zombie overnight? It was the comet, stupid!

O-1 / Olympia

Beware! This movie was made to be Nazi propaganda. Yet something unexpected happened at the 1936 Olympic Games— Jesse Owens! This black runner (who the NAACP tried to keep from coming to Berlin) ran all the white guys off the track and stole the show. And Leni Riefenstall made sure her cameras captured this cosmic moment in track history. To me, this movie is extra special since in high school track I ran some of the same races that Jesse broke records in.

O-5 / On Her Majesty's Secret Service

This is the quintessential James Bond caper—with Bond getting married! To Diana Riggs! In Switzerland, in the winter! As usual, plenty of action. But real sentiment as well, Bond as a human being.

O-14 / Our Man Flint

James Bond is a spoof of "spook" (secret agent) movies. Flint is a spoof of James Bond movies. Usually this kind of humor sags but they got this one right. Funny, lots of action, superb casting of James Coburn as Flint.

R-3 / The Russians are Coming, The Russians are Coming

I believe few movies have affected American audiences as this one did. I remember the audience's reaction because I could feel it and hear it. They were laughing and clapping. Not surprisingly, some critics downplayed it and could not understand why it was so popular.

I think it had subliminal "messages" it was broadcasting such as "we are all people, Americans and Russians alike," and maybe, "the common people are smarter and nicer than their leaders." Remember, this was made in 1966 at the height of the Cold War. In October of 1962, Americans and Russians (in the Cuban Missile Crisis) had come face to face with nuclear Armageddon, and the Russians had blinked and backed down.

I came across a "Viewpoints" opinion article in a major newspaper in September 2016, where James A. Haught, Editor Emeritus of West Virginia's *Charleston Gazette – Mail*, referenced this move in detail, arguing that it was about increasing human decency and compassion.

My collaborator, Joyce, had a more personal reaction, "That movie made me laugh for the first time in two years, since escaping my first marriage."

R-14 / RACE

This movie is about politics, race, young black athletes, Jesse Owens and the 1936 Olympic Games. It is about the difficult dilemma faced by Jesse Owens who is trying to decide whether to compete or to boycott Hitler's Berlin Olympics as the NAACP leaders urged him to.

Jesse did compete and brought home the gold—lots of it. He further embarrassed Herr Hitler by befriending one of the German sprinters (who was sent to the front lines a few years later for not beating Jesse). Even Leni Riefenstall is portrayed here, in this very fine movie.

If you want to see the "flip-side" of this movie, see "Olympia" where Leni's cameras record Jesse's real-life spectacular wins.

R-15 / THE RAZOR'S EDGE

This was one of Tyrone Power's better movies and was big in its day. It's the story of an earnest man's search for meaning. Not a theme that's timely today perhaps but an engrossing story and good acting. My stepfather, Juan Duval, was a character actor and had a short run-on part with Tyrone.

S-13 / THE SECRET OF SANTA VITTORIA

This is a delightful World War II tale and a fine example of a novel converted to movie with humor and worldview intact. Italians make good buffoons but beware of these Bobbolinos—they can fool you. And secrets can be kept if few people spill them. (That's a pun, see the movie.)

For my money this is the best horse race movie ever made. It's a dignified "women's liberation" themed movie as well and Disney did it all.

A woman whose father was a famous horse breeder and trainer enters the man's world of breeding racehorses. Her "pick," who is big and red, is laughed at. Secretariat starts running ever faster and faster; neither the owner or trainer know what the horse is capable of so they let it run its way—and track history is made.

S-29 / SECONDHAND LIONS

This movie is about family, honor and all that old-fashioned good stuff. A mother who is a self-centered, man-crazy, larcenous, no-account loser leaves her young son with his two great uncles, whom she thinks are ex-gangsters with a big stash hidden away at their Texas "farm." These two "secondhand lions" (played with exquisite finesse by Michael Caine and Robert Duvall) are two eccentric brothers who had a long career as professional soldiers of fortune. They could fill an Arabian tale book with their many adventures. They become good parents to the boy and even give him his own pet, a decrepit, ancient lioness who inhabits their cornfield. This is just for starters. This movie is bursting with life, humor, decent human beings, interesting slimeballs, and other interesting low-lifes. Duvall's oration to a young, teenage would-be thug is memorable scriptwriting reminiscent of Henry V's famous pre-battle speech. Don't miss this movie.

T-7 / The Thing

The later version of this movie had gorier special effects, but this early version (1950) feels closer to the horror of reading Don A. Stuart's classic short story "Who Goes There?"

U-1 / The Uninvited

An excellent adaptation of Dorothy McCardle's ghost/mystery novel of the same name, with decent human beings of an earlier era you can still relate to.

U-4 / A United Kingdom

This is a modern-day historical fairy tale romance set in Botswana. The heir to the country's throne marries a white woman and his uncle says, "No good." The ensuing factionalism splits the country and years of turmoil ensue. This is an awe-inspiring human story. For years it looks like it's two people against the whole world—of blacks and whites. A realistic human accommodation is finally reached: triumph of the human spirit and hope for our future.

V-2 / The Valley of Gwangi

This is a real off-beat movie. A mixture of cowboy, sci-fi and witchcraft.

Hollywood chose well because "Wizard" was the first of H. Frank Baum's books linking Kansas with the Land of Oz yet he wrote many others. He used both the characters in "Wizard" and new and entertaining eccentric others. Yet this rich, witty material with strong role models for young girls lies undisturbed while movie makers stumble over themselves to constantly remake old movies—most of which achieved perfection the first time. Like this one.

W-7 / The Wrong Box

A delightful adaptation of Geoffrey Napier's minor comic classic novel of the same name; a mistaken identity romp.

5

New Grist for the "Movie Mill"

Untapped Literary Sources

Crystal Singer by Anne McCaffrey

Killashandra is young, pretty and has years of musical training. What can she do? Then she learns about the Heptite Guild on the Planet Ballybran where Black Crystal is found, only by explorers with perfect pitch and unafraid of the dangers of "singing" crystal.

The Starmen of Llyrdis by Leigh Brackett

Michael Trehearne knew he was different from other men, but he didn't know why until he met that beautiful woman in a rural part of Brittany and learned the secret of the Vardda: the only "human" race that could withstand the rigors of true spaceflight.

Alpha Centauri or Die by Leigh Brackett

Earth has become one vast dictatorship. A group of scientists and technicians plan to escape by spaceship to Alpha Centauri (only 4.3 light years away)!

Sentenced to Prism by Alan Dean Foster

Evan Orgell, a confident company problem-solver, is sent to investigate why the company has not heard from their scientific laboratory on Prism, a beautiful planet. Instead of trees with bark, there are silicate creations. Even small animals look like living jewels. As Evan shortly finds out, they are beautiful but dangerous to carbon-based life forms.

Little Fuzzy, Fuzzy Sapiens by H. Beam Piper

On a remote planet, prospector Jack Holloway, discovers a tiny race of cute, fuzzy people. As you might expect this discovery upsets a lot of people and their development plans for this planet.

The Universe Against Her by James Schmitz

Telzey Amberdon is a super-smart, charming, and pretty college student. As the Psychology Service discovers, she has the potential to be the most powerful telepath ever known. Her adventures are thrilling and eerie. Here's another Women's Lib theme from the early days. (There are other Telzey books.)

The Demon Breed by James Schmitz

The protagonist of this book is yet another "superwoman" who is smart, athletic, fast-thinking, and knows how to play poker with the best of them. Her three friends are of both sexes but are large, intelligent, mutated otters. The invading Parahuans have a hard time trying to beat this team.

Star Rangers by Andre Norton

The first Galactic Empire is crumbling. Central Control is losing control. The Stellar Patrol's Vegan Scoutship Starfire is sent out on a desperate one-way mission to plot lost colonies and stars at galaxy's end. This is classic sci-fi at its finest. My opinion of Norton, an early sci-fi pioneer: She was the best, of the best of the best.

Hunters of the Red Moon by Marion Zimmer Bradley

This is a sci-fi rendering of a famous short story, "*The Most Dangerous Game.*" If you've never read it, then think of the movie "Predator." An alien people who like to hunt, set up an elaborate hunting contest (choose your weapon). The prize is your life (and great riches). A lizard man, a gentle female telepath, a female scientist/athlete, and an adventurous earthman with experience in samurai sword work team up. Some of them live.

Podkayne of Mars by Robert Heinlein

Heinlein's heavier side (Starship Troopers) is better known than his light and funny side as represented by both these entries. In

Podkayne, we have an adventurous Mars girl on her first trip in space. She's kidnapped on Venus and finds out about fairies who really exist and are not nice.

The Star Beast by Robert Heinlein

John Thomas has a large pet, sort of like a rhinoceros or triceratops. John thinks Lummox is really smart. Sergei Greenberg of the Department of Spacial Affairs thinks he's no smarter than a dog, but he becomes a problem when he starts doing strange things like eating their old Buick.

Ines of My Soul by Isabel Allende

This dramatic historical novel is about Ines Suarez, a towering figure in Chilean history. Ines, an uneducated seamstress back in her native Spain, comes to the New World (the 16th century) to follow her husband, a no-account but handsome soldier. She ends up helping, with her lover Pedro de Valdivia, to carve a new country out of this raw land, the home of the ferocious Mapuche; whose brilliant war leader nearly wipes out the Spaniards. This story is preserved for posterity in the famous epic poem, "*La Araucana*," published in 1578. The tour guides say the Mapuche statues in Santiago are the most popular tourist attraction in the town.

The First Hundred Years of Nino Cochise by A. Kinney Griffith

Nino Cochise was the grandson of the famous Cochise of the Chiricahua Apache. This bio history is a fascinating document. Nino bridges the time gap and culture gap. He is both a citizen of

Arizona and Mexico's Sierra Madre where he made local history and hid out for many years (as Apaches have historically done for hundreds of years). He had an adventurous life and ended up in California as an old man.

Conquistadors in North American History by Paul Horgan

Horgan was a historian. His bio of Cortez is a fascinating document. Much of Cortez's success was due to his military and intelligence officer (a brilliant, multilingual mistress who with her encyclopedic linguistic and cultural smarts enabled him to plot each of his moves toward the Emperor's Palace in Mexico City). A small part of this big story (the early part) was told in the movie, "The Captain from Castile."

The Blue Nile, The White Nile by Alan Moorehead

Either of these well-written histories offers a wealth of fascinating historical material for movies of historic adventure. For example, Napoleon's invasion of Egypt, the Mamelukes, etc. The movie "Khartoum" comes from this period.

The Nonesuch by Georgette Heyer

Although it would be like poaching, American movie makers could pull off doing one of the Regency novels of Georgette Heyer (one of England's favorite 20th century authors). After all, they did a great job with "Tom Jones," and some others. It would be a challenge. First of all, there's the problem of translating English into American. The term "nonesuch" means a super-dude kind of all-around guy (top athlete, man about town, etc.). In this book, Sir

Waldo Hawkridge quietly pursues Ancilla Trent, an unorthodox governess, whose young ward, Tiffany, is a smashing, young and inexperienced beauty who turns men's heads. As Bantam describes it: "A romantic comedy of manners set in England's elegant Regency Age."

Cotillion by Georgette Heyer

This is another of Heyer's books that is full of life, likable people, and zany characters. It's about "mistakes in love." *The Spanish Bride* is a bit different as it's about a British officer in the Napoleonic war period who takes a young Spanish lady as his wife as he fights in "*The Peninsula*."

The People of the Mist by H. Rider Haggard

Here's a terrific entry in the adventure genre. This is Haggard's search for lost jewels that does have a woman in the plot. In fact, there are two. One is the beautiful Juanna and the other is Soa, a fascinating lady who is Juanna's protector. The male protagonist, Leonard Outram, is an English adventurer and "Otter" is his friend (a black dwarf, disfigured but of immense strength). It is rubies they are after in the temple of the people of the mist. This is a great book. How could the movie makers go wrong?

Allan Quatermain

This is the actual sequel to "King Solomon's Mines." Alan Quatermain brought home the diamonds but later on lost the most valuable jewel, his son Harry. Harry was a young doctor in training who died of exposure to cholera while treating patients.

Quatermain is in mourning and wanders about in a funk until he meets his old friend, Umslopogaas, a deposed Zulu chieftain and a famous warrior. They travel about looking for the lost Zu-Vendi people (who don't want to be found). Two men who had nothing left—except their reputations. Alan, the older man, is still considered the best shot in Africa. His nickname among the natives is "He who watched by night", i.e. the sharpie you better steer clear of. This is a surprisingly touching story of two men from different races and cultures who like each other and can trust each other. Haggard was no dilettante. He knew the Zulu and Africa first hand and wrote extensively about conditions there.

Ozma of Oz, Glinda of Oz by L. Frank Baum

Baum wrote about twenty or so Oz books and they are all interesting to children of all ages. These two listed have a particularly strong feminist cast and provide strong, positive role models for young girls.

A Sort of Samurai by James Melville

Melville wrote nearly two dozen Superintendent Otani modern-day Japan mysteries (set mostly in the 80s). He was a Britisher who worked overseas in cultural diplomacy posts. In *A Sort of Samurai*, Otani who is chief of the Hyogo Prefectural Police, matches wits with Baron Bunsho Maeda, a right-wing criminal mastermind; with the able assistance of staff like Inspector Kimura and "Ninja" Noguchi. These books exhibit a deep understanding of Japanese attitudes and customs.

Murder in Canton by Robert Van Gulik

Van Gulik was a scholar-diplomat and expert on China. He wrote a series of Judge Dee murder mysteries set way back in China's Tang Dynasty period. There really was a Judge Dee in Chinese history and Van Gulik used the historical material as the foundation for the writing of sophisticated and entertaining stories set in their correct historical milieu.

Gold from Crete, The Captain from Connecticut by C.S. Forester

Many of Forester's novels have been successfully transferred to the screen but he wrote many other good books besides the Hornblower series. His book, *The Gun*, was made into the movie, "The Pride and the Passion." His *Gold from Crete*, is a World War II naval story. *The Captain from Connecticut* was the story of Captain Josiah Peabody, a hero of America's early Navy who was a successful blockade runner in the War of 1812.

The Doppelganger Gambit, The Dragon's Teeth by Lee Killough

This is a story of a futuristic police force where the cops are called "Leos" and the country's law and order lynchpin is a massive computer that keeps track of all citizens at all times. A starship broker commits drug suicide and Mama Maxwell thinks it's murder but Janna Brill, his partner, thinks it's legit. Janna is a "by the book" type. Maxwell is considered brain bent but occasionally brilliant. It's a great sci-fi mystery, followed by *The Dragon's Teeth*.

Sargasso of Space, Plague Ship by Andre Norton

Sargasso begins this two-part adventure of the Free Trader ship "Solar Queen." Captain Jellico, Cargo Master Van Rycke, Dane Thorson and others of the crew buy a planet at official auction. They find it's a planet that has an ancient "tractor" beam and attracts space ships and causes them to crash; they are being plundered by a ruthless outlaw organization (Jacks).

In *Plague Ship* a rich space combine (I-S) plants a dangerous pest aboard their ship causing them to be shunned as a plague ship; in order to break their trade monopoly on the Planet Sargol, home of the cat-like Salariki. This is inventive and delightful sci-fi at its best.

Pirate Latitudes by Michael Crichton

This is a swashbuckling pirate tale with a historical feel to it. Port Royal, capital of England's Jamaica territory in 1665, is the setting. Some of the pirate characters you've seen before, but others will surprise you. Captain Charles Hunter (aptly named for a privateer-pirate) is a latter-day Sinbad. Thirteen of Crichton's books have been made into movies—quite a batting average.

The Yorktown Campaign and the Surrender of Cornwallis by Henry P. Johnston

This is an important book on a little-known battle of our Revolutionary War; the one whose outcome in our favor enabled the United States of America to be founded. Yorktown was a tiny colonial village in tidewater Virginia. The long-range plan to trap Cornwallis (considered the best British general) was essentially George Washington's, and shows he was an intelligent military man not just a resolute one. Washington's army was backed up by his French allies, Infantry and Navy. It was this Allied Force that together defeated Cornwallis.

Ride the River, The Cherokee Trail, Last of the Breed by Louis L'Amour

This is a treasure trove of material. Although perhaps ten of his books have been made into movies, he wrote about 100! Some L'Amour movies—"Hondo," "Catlow," and "Conagher"—were pretty good. Others not so good. Westerns are not easy to make right. Here are some suggestions from his little-known books: *Ride the River* (from the Sackett series) and *Cherokee Trail*. Both of these are strongly feminist-themed books. Hollywood has lots of accomplished young actresses that would love to get a chance at the heroine-protagonists in either of these books. Oscar fodder!

In *Ride the River*, Echo Sackett does what has to be done when none of her menfolk are available to help. As the Bantam rear jacket says, "A sure hand with a horse, a dead shot with a rifle, and fast with her wits. Echo travels to the mountains of Tennessee, coming up against ruthless killers who would stop at nothing to cheat her of her inheritance."

Cherokee Trail takes place in wild Colorado Territory. Mary Breydon, her daughter Peg, and her husband head out that way because her husband has been hired to operate a stage station along a dangerous part of the Cherokee Trail route. Her husband dies in route and she and her daughter take the job on their own.

L'Amour didn't just write traditional westerns. In *Last of the Breed* he wrote about a modern-day Indian who had Air Force training as well as the survival skills of his people. This is a modern-day Cold War epic with our protagonist trying to bring back important military secrets after he is shot down in Siberia. And settling the score with those who tried to imprison him and break him.

Tales of the South Pacific by James Michener

There's a short story here entitled *The Landing on Kuralei*, that could be the basis for a sophisticated World War II movie. It's about Lt. Colonel Kenjuro Hyaichi, an honor graduate from Caltech, whose Japanese commander asks him to look at their island's likely invasion through the eyes of an American general, determine where the Americans will likely land, and how to prepare a defense for it. He succeeds—almost. Engrossing, real-life history. Shows the Japanese were not only good fighters but smart.

The Cassandra Group by Joseph A. Bonelli

This short eerie novella written by yours truly and published by Sunstone Press is an example of sci-fi—and specifically alternate history—used to address, or maybe toy with, some of our most intractable world political problems, such as the successful ending of the Korean War. It's clearly not over, with North Korea sill periodically sending off missiles in battle with a phantom enemy of the past. These out-of-date people are still dangerous like a ticking time bomb or an unexploded land mine. Those of our own history rewriters should take note of the current day dangers of tinkering with the past or obsessing over it. The image of President Trump as a diplomat strikes most people as ludicrous. Yet, no one has come closer to turning that strange man-boy Kim away from the dark side of vengeance toward the light side of Capitalist Satiation. But our extensive cultural differences got in the way after all. Que lastima! What a shame!

Mary Stewart's suspenseful and literate books, such as *Nine Coaches Waiting*, *Wildfire at Midnight*, and *My Brother Michael* are a must for movie-makers wanting to make superior movies with a shot at the Oscars.

Catherine Marchant's semi-gothics, such as *The Mists of Memory*, *Heritage of Folly*, and *Evil at Roger's Cross* are also good sources for stories about real and likable protagonists.

Another fine writer of the 1950s whose books have similar cinematic potential was Leslie Ford.

MOVIES THAT COULD BE REMADE

Why do I encourage doing movie "remakes" when elsewhere I've hinted they are a pain? Because some movie makers either misunderstood their literary source, chose to only use some of its plot, setting, etc. and its name recognition, or just plain botched it.

Let's back up. A movie that was done right the first time doesn't need to be remade; it's timeless, so to speak, so it doesn't need to be "reinterpreted" for new generations of moviegoers. "Planet of the Apes," "True Grit," and "Red Dawn" are such movies in my opinion but they were all remade. I believe all these remakes are inferior to the originals and most critics would agree.

Here comes a curveball. It's not always the first version that's the best. For "King Solomon's Mines" and "Last of the Mohicans" it was the second or later version.

King Solomon's Mines by H. Rider Haggard

Last of the Mohicans by James Fenimore Cooper

Here comes another curveball. Though I have rated these movies as classics, neither one of them comes close to having the full plot or an accurate understanding of the character of their protagonists in their literary sources listed above. Their plots and characters were "updated for modern tastes" and they were both bang up good jobs. Someone bold or foolish enough to try and portray these protagonists as their authors saw them should be allowed to do so because they will come up with something new and different.

As I explained earlier, "King Solomon's Mines" has no female in its plot and "Hawkeye" in both Mohican movies is nothing like Cooper envisioned him. To Cooper, Hawkeye was a "White Indian," someone who rejected his white culture (except for the rifle) and who "wouldn't pick up his cross" i.e. he rejected Christianity; he was a pagan and a revolutionary character. He consorted with Indians and preferred their company to that of white men.

A Connecticut Yankee in King Arthur's Court by Mark Twain

There have been multiple attempts to convert this serious classic American novel into a movie. From what I've read, none of these has come close. They are all playing games with the time travel gimmick. The first was a Bing Crosby 'musical'? A 1989 TV movie sent back a female singer, and a Disney movie a robot. Mark Twain, for all his humor, would not be laughing at what they did with the plot of his rather serious 'futuristic' novel. I would say the runway is clear for someone who wants to do it over—and get it right this time.

Movies that Were Remade—Sort of
(Special Editions or Director's Cut)

A word or two about "Special Editions" and "Director's Cut" movies. Beware and rejoice! Some movies have been changed substantively since their first release. Most such upgrades which have usually tinkered with the ending, have been worthwhile.

A trio of sci-fi flicks such as "Blade Runner," "The Abyss," and "Sphere" are illustrative. "Blade Runner" (the original) is a different movie than the Director's Cut (and I have listed both of them). I like them both. In the original, the android leader has a stemwinder of a speech and the ending is hard-edged. In the director's cut the ending is clever and humane, and the android's speech trimmed. In "The Abyss" Special Edition, the plot near the end has been drastically changed for the better (probably as originally intended). The ending of "Sphere" has been dramatically altered and it is not acknowledged by the movie makers. If, at the end, all is amity among scientists on the sphere, then you are seeing the new version. If you feel the ending has a tinge of horror, then you are seeing the original version. Again, I like them both.

Detailed Plot Dissection
of Ridley Scott's "Black Rain"

"Black Rain" is an extraordinary "cop-partners" action movie which begins on the streets of New York and ends in a rural farmhouse in Japan. The protagonists, a streetwise New York City cop and his younger partner (at the end of a trans-Pacific flight), are the victims of a clever bureaucratic ruse and deliver their Japanese Yakuza mobster prisoner not to the Osaka police as planned but to the mobster's own cronies.

Without badges and guns and in a two-country bureaucratic disgrace, they try to find him again with the help of an older English-speaking Japanese detective who is reluctantly assigned to help and keep them out of trouble. Some sly humor emerges, but the Japanese detective's English does not include New York street slang.

Maltin says this movie is "slick and entertaining"—and I agree, but Ridley Scott, who has an in-depth cross-cultural understanding of Japanese ways is up to much more and he pulls it off with the help of a superb cast of international actors. Perhaps he read the Superintendent Otani novels of brilliant scholar/diplomat James Melville?

To find his quarry, our New York City cop must learn how people think in Japan because the rules are different there especially in law enforcement. During this search, his younger New York City sidekick gets careless and dead. The Japanese detective, feeling guilty, uses one of his own country's customs to make amends—allowing the remaining friend of a pair bond their choice of a deceased friend's "keepsake." The "choosing keepsake box" includes the dead cop's gun.

In America, the land of rampant individualism, the cop partners "buddy bond" is strong. In Japan, conformity to the social group's goals is the overriding focus of an individual's every action. Trouble!

These differing views of honor and responsibility collide in a script that brilliantly captures the resulting mayhem. Our cop is more than macho tough, he is intuitive and streetwise smart, quickly understanding the new rules of the game, where the power is, and the Yakuza code.

As the search continues, the Japanese partner feels honor-bound to report to his superiors that he saw one of his New York City partners take several one hundred-dollar bills off a table in a raid which was aimed at finding the missing mobster. He did this (by burning them up) to test whether they were counterfeit (they were). The New York City cop believes his new partner would naturally cover for him until they could pow-wow. Before this conversation can take place, he is deported and placed on a plane for home. Desperate, our cop goes for it, escaping the plane and devising a long-shot plan based on his reading of Yakuza motivations. He wants a face-to-face with the area chief, the Yakuza boss, to whom the missing mobster is an embarrassment and threat. He figures this man will know where the fugitive is hiding. The cop understands his status as a "Gaijin" (stranger) gives him no status but his argument, "You have nothing to lose by helping me (to kill your rival)" is accepted; he is thrown a shotgun and shells).

Just in time! As the farm is about to be the locus of a big Yakuza gathering, the Japanese detective shows up to "go for it" and help his partner—but as a private citizen—since he has been fired from his job. Double-cross and violence unfolds for the action buffs. After it's over, the New York City cop and Japanese detective turn over the escaped mobster—alive—to the Osaka police.

As the New York City cop prepares to fly home, he exchanges presents (a Japanese tradition) with the detective who is still puzzled by his enigmatic friend and the things he says and does. Not sure he is totally honest the detective gets his answer when he opens his present; beneath the shirt there is something that can either make him rich or get him back on the police force. Find out for yourself. This is a great movie!

The same year this movie was released (1989), there was a Japanese movie released with the identical title. It was about a family that survived Hiroshima and the effects the radioactive fallout (which fell as black rain) had on them physically and emotionally. The chief Yakuza boss in the movie believed that all the bad things that had happened to Japan since they lost the war had come to them through the black rain of Western influence.

To the film buff with a long memory, the protagonist reminds me of Serpico, and the Japanese culture scene and Yakuza violence of this movie may have influenced the X-Men spinoff "Wolverine." Imitation is the sincerest form of flattery. Rest assured, Ridley did it right!

References

Leonard Maltin's 2007 Movie Guide. Plume. (Penguin Group) The last yearly Maltin was published in 2015. Expected future publications every five years.

VideoHound's Golden Movie Retriever. 2017. Project Editor Michael J. Tyrkus. c. Gale, Cengage Learning.

52 Must-see Movies and Why They Matter. (Turner Classic Movies). The Essentials, Jeremy Arnold. c. Turner Classic Movies, Inc. Published by Running Press.

Reading the Silver Screen. Thomas C. Foster. A Film Lover's Guide to Decoding the Art Form that Moves, Harper Perennial, 2016.

The Film Buff's Bucket List: The 50 Movies of the 2000s to See Before You Die. Chris Stuckman, Key Lime Press, Published by Mango Media.

1001 Movies You Must See Before You Die. General Editor, Steven Jay Schneider. A Quintessance Book, 2015, Published by Barron's Education Series, Inc.

Talking Pictures: How to Watch Movies, Ann Hornaday, Basic.

70 Years at the Movies. Edited by Ann Lloyd, Crescent Books, New York.

The Movies. Richard Griffith and Arthur Mayer, Bonanza Books, New York.

Fifty Years of the Movies. Jeremy Pascal, Exeter Books, New York.

Best. Movie. Year. Ever. (1999), Brian Raftery, Simon & Shuster.

About the Author

I became a movie lover in 1947 at the age of five when my father took me to the Verdi Theater in San Francisco's North Beach. Also at age five, Joyce acquired a movie mentor in her maternal grandmother who took her to movies in Berkeley. I completed some cinema and art history classes at UCLA in 1962 and nearly completed course work for a cinema major at USC in 1963 and 1964. I had family and friends in the movie business but none in high places.

My life path then made some abrupt turns. An empty wallet was one factor. I finished out at USC flat broke but debtless with a BA in Comparative World Literature and a heavy background in psychology, sociology, history, and science. I became a disability social worker then two years later did a six-month "Frommer frugal" solo tour of the US and Europe on my own with money saved while living at home.

After returning home I met and married Joyce, the love of my life (a Berkeley grad) who some years later I put through MSW grad school at Cal State, Sacramento. When she returned the favor I had a masters in Social Service Administration from the University of Chicago, including a semester as a presidential intern in the Swamp.

I worked in Policy and Research for the U.S.D.A. in the Washington DC "big pond" where I was a small fish for ten years before returning west were the sun shines more. Joyce ended up as a psychotherapist for the Air Force.

Throughout the following years, my wife and I continued our movie-going avocation. When we retired, we embarked on a grand journey of rediscovery by looking at our old favorite movies. Most, but not all, still looked good.

Then we embarked on a years-long search for new movies, even those that had been "scrubbed" by the critics. We found gold, old and new! This book is the fruit of that search.

I hope this book helps moviegoers, especially the young ones like our granddaughters, Sophia and Samantha, to discover that some of the finest movies ever made were filmed before they were born.